Praise for Make Money Your Honey

"Money. We need it, we want it, we never seem to have enough of it. Amanda has taken this difficult topic and shifted our mindsets around it. If you're ready to value yourself and your business, learn how to attract abundance, and go on a date with your money - then Make Money Your Honey is a must-read. I couldn't put it down."

—Diana Antholis, Author and Lifestylelist, dianaantholis.com

"If you're ready to change the way you think about work and money once and for all and finally start calling in the abundance you deserve, then this book is a must read. At such a young age, Amanda truly understands the universal truths about such an important topic and shares practical tips that everyone can benefit from in their financial lives."

- Brittney Castro, Certified Financial Planner and Founder & CEO of Financially Wise Women

"I truly believe that entrepreneurship is the new 'job security' for Gen Y and this books captures that brilliantly. Many books on money focus on cutting your expenses but this book focuses on growing your career - which I loved!"

- Sophia Bera, CFP®, GenYPlanning.com

MAKE MONEY YOUR HONEY

A SPIRITED ENTREPRENEUR'S GUIDE
TO HAVING A LOVE AFFAIR WITH
WORK & MONEY

AMANDA ABELLA

MAKE MONEY YOUR HONEY

A SPIRITED ENTREPRENEUR'S GUIDE
TO HAVING A LOVE AFFAIR WITH
WORK & MONEY

Copyright © 2013 Amanda Abella

First Edition

ISBN: 978-0-615-93552-2

Amanda Abella, LLC

www.amandaabella.com

Become a member of Amanda's FIRE Tribe
community for free and receive:

Set Fire to Your Goals Video Workshop

And

Fierce Fireball Kit

The Workshop and Kit Include:

- Full length video of the Set Fire to Your
Goals group coaching workshop

- 30 Day Set Fire to Your Goals Guide

- Start That Side Hustle Guide: Freelancing
in Your Post-Grad Life

- Goals Are Dreams with Expiration Dates:
5 Steps to Stop Thinking and Start Doing

Access it by visiting:

www.amandaabella.com/join-the-tribe

*Dedicated to all of those who want to create
a career that fits seamlessly into their lives.*

CONTENTS

PART TWO
DON'T CONVINCE;
CONTRIBUTE!

PART THREE
MONEY: FROM "OH SHIT!"
TO "I GOT THIS!"

Go Make That Money, Honey!

Preface

Loving what we do for a living.

This elusive statement seems like a dream these days. We all aspire to love our work. We all want to wake up in the morning and enjoy what we do. But so few people actually achieve this.

We have an automatic tendency to think that work, and especially money, need to be difficult. We tend to believe that we cannot make money doing what we love. Yet we also believe that once we figure out The Secret, win the lottery, or get lucky that all that stuff will sort itself out.

It won't; because here's the deal: as with everything in life, the secret to having a love affair with your work and your money comes totally from within.

Because at the end of the day all we really want is to be happy.

To make sure we're provided for.

To feel good about the work that we do.

To wake up in the morning and not dread another work day.

To look at our bank accounts without clenching our jaws.

To have the guts to pursue what we love.

To spend money on the things and people we love.

To give back and help those around us.

To leave our mark on the world.

To trust ourselves.

To have confidence.

To allow ourselves to show our authenticity - no gimmicks, no facades, and no games.

To feel comfortable, in control, and like its all good when it comes to work, money, and ultimately our lives.

After years of letting myself be affected by negative money stories, overworking myself to the bone, and putting my personal life on the back burner, I can finally say that I've created work I love, get paid for it, and actually enjoy taking care of my finances.

My life is no longer revolving around my job. Quite the opposite, my career fits seamlessly into my life so I can show up for others, enjoy what I do on a daily basis, take care of myself, and have a hell of a good time.

Though this can totally happen overnight, chances are it won't (it sure didn't for me). The tools and mental shifts I outline in this book are techniques I still use daily to keep myself in check. In fact, I find that the more I grow my business and learn about finances, the more I use the techniques outlined in this book. However, I do promise that with enough practice everything in this book will start becoming second nature

My Story

"If opportunity doesn't knock, build a door"

— *Milton Berle*

In May of 2010 I was a broke college graduate who moved back home. It was the same year that infamous New York Times article, *What Is It About 20-Somethings?*, created quite a stir.

By that article's standards I was just another statistic. I was another directionless millennial with no aspirations, had a penchant for taking pictures of my food, and had a nasty sense of entitlement.

Except I really wasn't any of those things - I'd just been screwed over by the Recession. You try finding a job when your hometown's unemployment rate is upwards of 13%.

Everything I'd been told since I was a child - go to school, get decent grades, go to college, and find a good job - had gone up in smoke. There were countless articles, stories, and statistics out there about how screwed my generation was.

How we'd never make enough money. How 80% of 2010 college graduates had to move back in with their parents. How student loan debt would ruin us because we couldn't find decent jobs. How we'd never amount to anything at all.

To say that I had anxiety over all of this would be an understatement. I remember having a panic attack in my parent's kitchen because I honestly had no idea what I was doing with my life. Eventually you just throw your hands up in the air and wonder if there was ever any point to anything. This is the moment when one of two things happen - either you give up and just let things happen to you, or you're cracked open with new possibilities.

Fortunately for me, it was the latter. I read two books that summer that completely changed my life. The first was The Dalai Lama's *Art of Happiness*. I was wandering aimlessly in a book store and gravitated toward the Philosophy and Religion section.

I've had a fascination with this stuff since I was a child and thought *Art of Happiness* was a pretty gutsy title. So I bought it.

This book immediately changed the way I saw obstacles in life. I had an awakening and felt the kind of faith in life and miracles I only remembered having as a child. This book has been so instrumental in my life that I think everyone should have it on their book shelf.

The second book was the real kicker. A good friend of mine handed me Chris Guillebeau's *Art of Non-Conformity*. In case you haven't heard of this, Chris Guillebeau basically wrote a manifesto on how we don't have to do things the way we've been told. We've each got *carte blanche* in this life and it would be in our own best interest to use it. I was sold.

I didn't realize it at the time, but the seed had been planted for a major quantum shift in my own life - one where I realized that work, money, and life didn't have to be so damn difficult. One where everything could work seamlessly together to create a spectacular life.

I slowly started to believe that I didn't have to wait for someone to give me a job, I didn't have to be stupid with whatever money I made, I could make as much money as I wanted regardless of where the Dow was, and I sure as hell didn't have to sit at an office desk for 30 years while I counted down to retirement.

An entrepreneur was born. I hopped on to Wordpress, started a blog called Grad Meets World, began freelance writing as a means of making money, and things slowly started to shift.

This was a very slow process because I had no idea what my ideal work and life looked like. I also had zero business chops (I was a Literature major after all) and still had some major work to do in the money department. So like any responsible person, I did work at regular office jobs for quite some time while I figured out my life's work on the side.

One job in particular not only gave me the business chops I needed, but also helped me witness a very serious problem among working professionals:

There is a major disconnect for people when it comes to work, money, and happiness.

Common Beliefs About Work and Life

I worked for a small job placement agency that specialized in finding candidates for entry level positions within Fortune 500 companies.

I did the math my last week on the job and realized I had interviewed close to 2,000 people for jobs within some of America's top companies.

I also realized that the majority of these people were not happy. Some sabotaged incredible opportunities. Others shared stories about how their demanding jobs destroyed their relationships. College grads were battered and bruised as they realized that most of the stuff they'd been told in school about "the real world" didn't apply in a tough job market. Their health was down the tubes as companies tried to do more with less people. And almost everyone was freaking out about money. Even people making six figures were broke.

People had become totally disconnected. They assumed that work and money had to be filled with struggle - and that's inevitably what they would get.

I vowed to never become one of these people. I also vowed to help others avoid this same kind of fate. So I plugged away at my blog, got my life coaching certification, and actively worked on my own beliefs about work, money, and how they related to life.

With the techniques I learned from classes, teachers, mentors, and my own life I started creating a career that I loved and allowed me to do what I wanted - travel, work with incredible people, and have fun. Best of all, I did this without scrimmaging for money, living under a bridge, or forgoing a retirement account.

I also started applying these techniques on fellow students, clients, and readers and was happy to see that they too started making some radical shifts in their own careers, bank accounts, and lives.

I knew I was on to something - but it would take me a little while longer before I could live out my ideal business and teach others to do the same.

Burning Out Turns Into Blazing On

By the time December 2012 came around I was kind of a hot mess. I was working full time at an employment agency and I'd been trying to build a business on my own for two and a half years.

After a summer relationship didn't work out I went at everything full force. A part of me (call it intuition) knew I'd been given a green light to finally make my business a reality so that's what I tried to do.

Double the work at my full time job.
Blogging. Writing clients. Coaching clients.
Coaching classes. In person networking
events. Online networking events. Email
lists. Interviews. You name it.

I kept pushing and clawing, giving up
sleep and a social life, working through
weekends, and still felt like I wasn't making
any headway.

I was making some income from my
own endeavors but it was sporadic from
month to month - eventually capping out at
about $1,000 a month.

I had a ton of support and people
interested in working with me but couldn't
quite figure out how to turn them into
paying clients.

I knew I had a bunch of good ideas but
couldn't find the common denominator.

In short, I had to done a lot of the mental
work that comes with being an entrepreneur
- actively working on changing my story and
beliefs - but I hadn't quite yet figured out
the practical side. You know, like, getting
paid.

I had become exactly what I wanted to
avoid - a slave to work and money. My
personal life was put on the back burner and
I was running myself into the ground.

Worst of all, I knew I was close. Really close. It was almost infuriating to know I was on the verge of something amazing and couldn't figure out what the hell it was. I was so burnt out and tired that I couldn't even remember Christmas 2012.

On December 31st, 2012 I had a major moment where I was very close to just quitting. I had a job, I could just find another at some point, and the easiest thing to drop would have been this incessant urge to work for myself and make money on my own terms. Right?

Wrong. I knew deep in my bones that finding another job would not make me feel better. I knew I would just end up in the same predicament all over again - overworking myself and having my life, schedule, and money decided by someone else.

It's just something I wasn't cool with. At that moment I knew I had the chops to make this happen and the only things stopping me were my own thoughts, beliefs, and behaviors.

It was time to kick it up a notch and I decided 2013 would be the year I finally made the leap. So I did something quite radical for a Type A go-getter. I started asking for help and investing in myself.

I hired my own coach. I actually started talking about what it is I did without feeling like a fraud. Asked for referrals and shares. I put on my first speaking event which led to the second and third. I started landing paying clients for writing and coaching. Most of all, I took a good honest (and hard) look at money - because if I wanted to pursue my life's work and live on my own terms, there was no way around it.

Amanda Abella

How to Use This Book

Keep these principles in mind as you work through the exercises in this book. Each section will require mental shifts about work and money. These shifts are then accompanied by practical questions and exercises to help you create or propel your own sacred business forward.

Each section of the book leads into the next in order to help you clear up what I call your money onion. Simply put, facing your financial fears can be a lot like peeling an onion. It requires different layers, starting on the surface and then getting deep into the work. It may also make you cry. However, once the onion is peeled you can use it to add flavor to the rest of your life.

*From Employee to Entrepreneur: Forget
Everything You Know About a Work Day*

If you understand that you are an
entrepreneur providing value for the world
you'll soon realize there is no need to slave
over your work or waste time on things that
won't actually make you any money.

Don't let people tell you that
entrepreneurs must work twice as much as
their office dwelling counterparts. Don't let
people tell you its too difficult and unstable.
And certainly don't let people tell you that
entrepreneurs don't have any work life
balance.

Don't Convince; Contribute!

Sales don't have to be awkward, scary,
or slimy. By becoming clear on who you
serve, what problems you fix, and what
value you provide for people you can
change lives without feeling like crap when
you ask to get paid.

You will also realize that the traditional
way of viewing competition is dead. We're
moving into a new economy of collaboration
and sharing.

Money: From "Oh Shit!" to "I Got This!"

The thing about money is that everyone has an opinion, but that doesn't mean someone else's story has to be your own. Similarly, looking at your finances and making them work for your given situation can be as fun, sexy, and exciting as a new boyfriend (or, girlfriend for the fellas reading this). They can also be as respectful, solid, and faithful as a lifetime partner regardless of how much you are raking in.

These are the philosophies that are covered in depth throughout the book, explaining exactly what they are, my story as well as those of clients in relation to them, and how to actually start taking some action toward pursuing your life's work without having to freak out about money.

Make Money Your Honey

Part One

Employee to Entrepreneur: Forget Everything You Know About a Work Day

Employee to Entrepreneur: Forget Everything You Know About a Work Day

Since the Recession the American economy has seen a major trend. More and more people are leaving traditional jobs and working for themselves as freelancers, contractors, consultants, business owners, and any other name you can come up with for the self-employed.

Intuit released their *2020 Report* in the midst of the Recession. In this report they claimed that if trends continued 40% of the

American workforce would be self-employed by 2020.

The Freelancers Union, one of the biggest advocacy groups for the self-employed, regularly claims that over 42 million Americans are already self-employed. To give you an idea that's about one third of the American workforce.

In my own adventures as a blogger, freelancer, and businesswoman I've also seen this trend increase in recent years. At first people were either forced into a situation where they had to work for themselves or found it by accident. Others became completely fed up with the practices of the traditional workplace and used that anger to fuel their own passions. Now, it's kind of the cool thing to do and seen as a viable option for many people.

It seems that every single networking event or workshop I go to - whether it be for nailing job interviews or marketing - has more and more entrepreneurs. Even people with regular jobs all have some kind of side endeavor these days.

I recently went to a workshop dedicated to helping people write resumes. Each and every single person in that workshop had their own business on the side. It almost made me wonder why we were even talking about resumes to begin with.

I personally think this is absolutely amazing! More and more Americans are realizing that they can create meaningful work they love and get paid for it. Unfortunately, many times they don't realize exactly what they've gotten themselves into. Let's be real here; working for yourself is a whole different ball game than working for someone else.

One of the biggest struggles I see with my clients is when they take their Employee Mentality into their business. That is to say, they take a lot of the same structures and ideas they had at regular jobs and then apply them to their own businesses. Sometimes this works. Most of the time it doesn't.

Here's the deal: we need to change our mentality about work if we're to run profitable businesses and create lives we love. Often times this also includes changing our mentality about ourselves.

The reality is that when it comes to your own business you're no longer an employee. In fact, that's exactly what we want to avoid - otherwise what's the point of working for yourself?

The Breakdown

Employee: Someone is telling you what to do, where to be, and when. You trade hours for dollars. Lots of structure. Your

17

lunch hour is decided for you. Customer is always right.

Entrepreneur: You make your own schedule. Trade value for dollars. More flexibility. You call the shots. You are the boss. You only work with ideal clients.

Here's what happens if you bring your Employee Mentality into your business:

- Your clients turn into your bosses; so instead of having to deal with one manager you now have several.

- You put in crazy hours on tasks that won't actually make you any money.

- You spend more time on paperwork, branding, design, and reading study materials than actually taking any action.

- You get stuck to definitions, not action.

- You're way too worried about technical business stuff instead of actually landing clients.

- You're working from a place of "busyness" not business.

Any of this sound familiar yet?

I thought so. It's cool. I totally get it. It took me ages to get it together in this department. I kept stressing over what my business should look like, how many hours I was putting into it, and dealing with crappy clients.

It's all because although I really wanted to run my own business I hadn't yet made the serious mental shift it required: seeing myself as a businesswoman.

You ARE an Entrepreneur

When someone asks you what you do for a living what to do you tell them? Are you still saying "Oh, well, I'm a [insert day job here]? And on the side I work on this thing that's kind of cool." Are you still fumbling as you try to find the words to explain what it is you actually do?

I did that for ages. I did that with friends, dates, strangers, at networking events, you name it. In fact I think my mom was the only person who actually knew what I was doing - and she probably didn't get it half the time.

I had this false belief that since I wasn't making a certain amount of money or it didn't look a certain way then I couldn't call myself an entrepreneur. Sure, it may have been plastered all over my blog, but the reality was I didn't believe it half the time. I thought someone would catch on to the fact that half of what I was talking about didn't even exist yet.

I'm going to teach you how to scratch that record; because here's the frank truth:

If you are trading money for goods or services, even if it's a few bucks, you are legally a business. Which means YOU ARE ALREADY AN ENTREPRENEUR.

There's no waiting until you make X dollars to consider yourself an entrepreneur. Your business doesn't have to look like anything for you to call it a business. You are not a fraud for being financially responsible and working a day job while you get your business off the ground. You are not any less capable or worthy of making money just because things don't look a certain way.

YOU ARE AN ENTREPRENEUR

And it's about time you start thinking like one, because it will change the way you see everything about work, money, and life.

IDENTIFYING YOUR BELIEFS EXERCISE

Exercise 1: What limiting beliefs are keeping you from calling yourself an entrepreneur? Get honest!

Examples may include: I'm not making a boat load of cash yet. I'm not as successful as X Person. I'm not qualified or certified. No one is paying me for my services.

Recognize that this all a bunch of poppycock. Our beliefs affect the way we see the world, not the other way around. By identifying your current blocks you can start working toward changing them *into empowering beliefs.*

MANTRA EXERCISE

Exercise 2: Create a mantra for yourself.

A mantra is a word or phrase that serves as a grounding tool whenever your mind goes astray. Create something that will remind you of your power as an entrepreneur. Put it as a reminder on your phone, stick a post-it to your computer, put it on a vision board, do whatever you can to make sure you see it often. Every time any thoughts of self-doubt arise recite your mantra to ground you.

Trade Value (Not Time) for Money

When I started my business I thought I had to put in 40 hours for it to mean anything. The result was that I was working 80 hour weeks between my regular job and the business where I'd become an employee.

The reality is that this structure of the 40+ hour work week doesn't necessarily work.

First of all, who actually puts in a full eight hour day marathon of productivity at a regular job? No one.

In fact, our brains literally can't handle it. We already know that we all check out and become distracted after a few hours of actual work. We also have doctors, health experts, and productivity gurus telling us to take more breaks so we can recharge.

Yet for some reason we insist on trying cram in all our work into a confined structure of 40 hours throughout a 5 day period. We have a false belief that this will make us productive and successful.

Why? First, we're programmed to think this way since most of society is going by this schedule. Second, at regular jobs we're trading time for money. Not productivity, not output, but time.

How often are you perusing Facebook and twiddling your thumbs at the office instead of actually working? You'll still get your paycheck because you're trading your time. Are you producing output during your time at your desk? Sure, but when you really think about it you're not really getting your base pay because of it.

In fact, how often have we found ourselves doing practically nothing at an office job yet we're still confined to our desks? If the work is done, why can't we just go home? The answer is because it would affect our pay. That is a perfect example of how we've come to trade our valuable precious time for a buck.

When you're a business owner you are no longer trading time. You literally can't afford to obsess over how many people are following you on Twitter or what paperwork you should invent to track your leads - there's also no reason why you should have to.

The beauty of this whole self-employment thing is that you can create whatever you'd like. For example, if you don't feel like LinkedIn is working for your business, then stop using it! No one is forcing you to do anything you don't want to do. You can also take breaks whenever you need to, take days off on a whim, travel, and work when you actually want to.

As my friend and colleague Diana Antholis so brilliantly put in her book *Unleashed: Live the Balanced, Centered, and Sexy Life You Deserve*, all us entrepreneurs know that we can get all the real work we need done in three hours.

How do we do this? By learning how to trade value, not time, for money.

Sure Fire Signs You're Still Trading Time for Money in Your Business:

- **Working for an hourly rate instead of per project or per package.**
  (Hourly rate is ok depending on what you do, but it's kind of hard to gauge how long a project will take and then charge a deposit for it - and yes you

should always have a deposit or just ask for payment upfront.)

- **Spending an eternity stuck in development instead of actually launching something.** (Example: Not giving yourself deadlines.)

- **Spending more time writing emails and freaking out over your bank account than talking to people.** (How exactly are you going get a client if you're not talking to people?)

- **Choosing projects based on a whim instead of what is actually right for your business at this point in time.**

- **Putting in 14 hour days because you feel like you have to, not because you are inspired to.**

In the spirit of transparency I'm going to be totally honest here: I still struggle with the time thing. It's a serious bad habit that many of us have to break, regardless of whether we're working at regular jobs or running our own businesses.

In my case, I spent so many years overworking myself that I still sometimes find myself repeating the same bad patterns in my own business. I've gotten much better about this thanks to the exercises and tips in this book, but it is something I have to regularly practice. If you find that you also tend to overwork yourself, don't sweat it! It will get better with time.

The primary steps in breaking the chains are to first value yourself and then figure out what value you are providing for people.

What the do I mean by value?

As the brilliant Kate Northrup puts it in her lectures and her book, money is just a stand-in for what we value.

Her theory is simple: we made money up. It's a system we created to exchange value for value.

For example, you go into a store and find a killer pair of shoes. You trade money you've (hopefully) already earned for the shoes if you find them to be worth that value. So, let's say the shoes were $500. I would not buy them because I don't value shoes in accordance with that price tag. Someone else on the other hand, most likely the designer's ideal client, would buy those shoes because they value shoes at that price.

Catch my drift?

So if you want more money for your business you need to start thinking in terms of value - both for yourself and for your business.

How to Start Valuing Yourself

Here's where it takes some major inside work: if you don't value yourself first then you can't give your best value out into the world through your business. Furthermore, if you don't value yourself and what you are offering you're going to have a hard time getting paid.

Most people go through their lives thinking very little of themselves. For some it's just in certain areas, for others it's all around.

So now I ask you, how can you expect to make the money doing something you want if you don't even believe you are providing any value into the world?

By not charging what you're worth, by not valuing your time, by not getting out there and talking to potential clients you're essentially just keeping yourself small. You are also totally disrespecting potential clients who are looking for a certain caliber of value.

Bottom line: if you want to get it together when it comes to work and money, you need to get it together with yourself.

It's often times I see entrepreneurs who don't give themselves enough credit. One client in particular was working on some sales copy for her free offering. She had done a great job of explaining her ideal client's angst and explaining what she does.

We looked over it together and I noticed something: nowhere in the copy had she described how amazing she is at what she does. Since I had taken her up on one of her sessions I knew she was really good - but she wasn't telling anyone!

Sure, she had testimonials which are great - fantastic even! But there was still something missing and you could tell from reading it. There was nothing there about why SHE was the one people should hire.

If you want to take your sales copy or even your pitch from vanilla to rockstar status you must tell people why YOU are the right person for the job. Show them results front and center!

This client in particular took spectacular client stories and put them on top of the page as a way of acknowledging her amazing clients and acknowledging herself for helping them get there. Most of all, it shows potential clients why she's the right person for them to hire!

There are other ways you can show how amazing you are. For instance, I've had clients whose works have been featured in magazines and big time publications - but I would have had to get to the third paragraph of their bio to even know that. By working together we came up with bios that exemplified their skills and showcased their results.

It's Okay to Toot Your Own Horn Every Once in a While

I'm all about being humble and being of service, but there is absolutely nothing wrong with owning how good you are at something. We all have gifts in this life and it's our job to share them with the world.

We confuse silence with modesty. Modesty still allows you to share your gifts when merited. Believe me, if you're trying to put a roof over your head, it's merited.

We also confuse confidence with conceit. Confidence is when we are able to recognize we're good at something while still allowing room to grow. Conceit thinks it can do no wrong. Big difference.

Here's an example to show you what I mean. If you were to go to a sales page and at the bottom is says, "If you're not willing to pay this much then you're just not ready to be awesome" you've crossed the line into conceit. You may be good enough to charge a lot of money and that's more than okay, but you've just alienated potential clients by acting like a jerk and not keeping their needs in mind.

On the other hand, if at the beginning of your sales page you have results like "My clients have done x, y, and z. And you can be one of them." you are showing potential clients just how amazing you are while inviting them to have fun.

It's time to rise up to our gifts, share them with the world, and start getting paid for them! Believe it or not, others expect nothing less from you, so why continue to sell yourself short?

Below you'll find some questions to help you identify what you're good at, how you can start letting potential clients know, and where you may still be holding back.

SELF VALUE EXERCISE

Answer the following questions:

What is it that you do very well?

Where in business (or life) have you excelled?

What is something you are proud of yourself for?

How can you show potential clients how amazing you are?

Where are you de-valuing yourself in terms of your business? Are you not charging enough? Are you working crazy hours for not enough money?

Get honest! The first step in fixing it is witnessing it. Don't worry if you find that you don't really like some of your answers. You also shouldn't worry if acknowledging yourself for the good work you've done feels uncomfortable. It's something we're not totally used to as a society. With daily practice of acknowledging your accomplishments it will get a lot easier.

How to Start Providing Value through Your Business

The second part of this equation is learning about what is valuable for your business. This is a twofold process: figuring out what you can do in terms of time and money, but also starting to realize what your clients actually need.

Essentially what you must learn is how to work smarter, not harder. You must also learn to always take your clients into account. This is the part where you start realizing that although certain boundaries are put in place to protect you (such as what you charge and your policies), at the end of the day it's not all about you.

You have to remember that you are no longer being paid based upon how many hours you put into something. All of your decisions - from working with ideal clients to deciding which project to take on ask two very important questions:

- Can my service/product serve this person to the best of my ability?

- Is this the right person for my business?

When you work with the right people you do your best work - and you actually enjoy doing it. These are the people you can provide the most value for and will in return provide the best value for you. Trust me, you'd much rather want to work with the right people who will become raving fans and send referrals your way (more on that later.)

This is in contrast to what many of us have been taught to believe. We're taught that the customer is always right. Real talk, no they're not. We also don't have to take on every project or person that comes in the door - especially if they are only going to bring on headaches.

We'll dive into figuring out who your
idea client is later on. For now just keep this
in mind: you do your best work when you
work with the best people.

Actually enjoying work. What a concept,
right?

You also need to be smart about what
projects you take on next. We need to make
sure our own cups are filled so that we can
serve others to the best of our ability, and
that requires dealing with money.

For instance, I'm constantly getting
requests to write for other websites for free.
A couple of years ago this would have been
fine because I was trying to build my
expertise in the area of work and money.
Now it's a totally different story.

I realized that the return on investment
wasn't worth the effort I was putting into it -
as such I cut this out and had more time on
my hands to work on things that my current
and potential clients would find valuable
while still allowing myself to get paid.

When in doubt, ask yourself the
following question:

- Can this actually grow my business
  and increase my revenue in an efficient
  way?

My girl Brandy Morris, creator of *Operation Ideation*, is a whiz at figuring this stuff out so I asked her to say a few words on the topic:

"Making the right move for your business requires a mix of input from the heart, brain, and gut. First and foremost, a business move should speak to your heart. If it doesn't excite the hell out of you or solve a problem that you're excited to see resolved, there's really no point is there? If you're a yes there, then you can go ahead and dive a little deeper in the head and gut stuff.

The brain needs to check for alignment. Choose ideas that speak to the needs of your people and steer your business in the direction you're headed. Make sure it plays to your strengths or comfortably stretches your skill set. Determine if you have the skills and resources needed to pull this off (focus on facts and actually do the math to avoid letting fear cloud your better judgment). Then it's finally time to give your gut the final word; it always knows best in the end."

I experienced this on a very visceral level not too long ago. When I quit my job to pursue my business I was doing one on one coaching. I thought the next logical step would be group coaching even though my heart was really saying "Your people need a book."

I ignored the intuition because after many attempts at writing something I just couldn't get into the topics I was choosing to write about. I also thought group coaching would be the next logical money making step for my business.

After talking with fellow entrepreneurs who'd recently quit their jobs I had an idea hit me like a sack of bricks - a group coaching course dedicated to helping people in vocational limbo - those who were so close to quitting their day jobs but needed an extra push. I asked people who were in this situation what they were struggling with. When I started developing this program I ended up with enough content for a book draft.

With more research and modifying that draft eventually turned into this book you're reading. It may not be about quitting your day job, but it is about rocking work and money regardless of whether you're a full time entrepreneur or a side hustler.

Group coaching would have been great, and it's definitely on the horizon, but I intuitively knew what my people wanted even if I wasn't so clear on the message off the bat.

As for the practical side of all of this, I also knew having a book would benefit my business growth as I participate in more conference panels and put on more speaking engagements. And finally, my coaching clients can use this book as a refresher whenever they want while newer readers (or those who aren't ready to spend a lot of money on coaching) can get a pretty thorough introduction into who I am and what I do.

There are two points to my story. The first is that when I was trying to write a book based on what *I* wanted to write about, rather than what my people were telling me they needed, I hated it. The second is that even though I intended to go in another direction with the quit your day job group coaching, I was inevitably led right back to where my intuition knew I needed to go.

Listen to your people and trust your gut. Works every time.

Forget the Frame, It's All about Content

In late 2012 I discovered a lot about reframing your thoughts by stumbling upon the work of Gabrielle Bernstein. She teaches a book called *A Course in Miracles*, which is all about mind training and reframing perspectives in your life.

One of my favorite lessons from the course is to focus on the content instead of the frame. It's a lesson that works with personal relationships, careers, and especially running your own business.

If you're too busy worried about logos, filing for legal papers before you have income, how many emails you're sending out and how your Facebook page looks you are wasting time. This is the frame - what something looks like. What you should be worried about is the content - what you provide, talking to people, being of service to those you are meant to help, and how it makes you feel.

Frame Mindset:

- Should I file for an LLC off the bat? (Well, if you don't have paying clients you can safely assume you shouldn't spend $200+ bucks yet.)

- Do I have to write blog posts 3 times a week? (Do you want to? Does it help your business grow? Can you even spend the time on that much content?)

- What about my logo? (How about you actually get on the streets and talk to people so you can pay for the logo design?)

- How many Twitter followers do I have? (If you're not talking to the actual people, it doesn't matter.)

Content Mindset:

- How the service you are providing makes you feel. (Does it inspire you? Can you work on it? Does it give you energy?)

- What value am I providing for my clients? Is this actually helping them?

- Talking to people and spreading the message.

- How can you better serve your people? (You won't know unless you ask them.)

Point is, as an entrepreneur you can stop worrying about the technical stuff so much. You will figure it out as you go along - I've rebranded three times since 2010 and I'm sure it'll happen again. Instead focus on the actions that will actually grow your business.

Actions like going to networking events and inviting ideal clients to some offer, talking to your readers one on one, joining entrepreneurial groups, and asking your clients how you can better serve them.

Notice how I've said nothing about content marketing, Facebook fans, Twitter followers, or using LinkedIn. All that stuff is fine and dandy, but like I said, if you're not actually *talking* to people you're going to have a hard time earning any income and leaving your mark on this world. Furthermore, as I previously mentioned, if you don't think that any of these things are helping your business then there's no reason why you should keep doing them.

Learning How to Say No

I have yet to meet an entrepreneur (or person for that matter) who never had to deal with learning how to say no.

We feel bad for saying no. We think we're being unkind. We think we should say yes to everything because anything could be the next big thing for our business.

I believe there are two things behind this phenomenon of not being able to say no: first, we feel bad because we want to please people and have them like us. Second, there's a false sense of urgency that if you miss just one opportunity you may have ruined your business forever.

Poppycock.

Here's what happens if you don't learn how to say no in business and in life:

- You become overworked and stressed with way too much on your plate.

- You go back to wasting time on things that may not actually move your business forward.

- You spend money on things you shouldn't be spending money on.

- You put yourself on the back burner.

I want to be very clear here, this does not mean we say no to everything. Lord knows saying yes to things has certainly propelled my business forward. Three years ago when I was just starting to embark on this journey and only had a fuzzy idea of what was happening I said yes to almost every opportunity that came my way. I was still in the very beginning stages and it was okay to say yes.

Saying yes when it was necessary helped me tailor my audience, craft my voice, test the waters in a bunch of different things, and get exposure. People used to ask me to write for free all the time and I'd do it. I've spoken for free at schools and events. I even coached for free during my certification process. If there was some sort of training program or course that I thought would teach me about online business I'd buy it, no questions asked.

All of these things really helped me figure out what I was meant to do and what I wasn't meant to do.

However, there comes a time when you can no longer do this. Not because it's not worth your time or because you're better than doing things for free every once in a while, but because we only have so much energy to give before we become completely depleted. Once we start growing and moving into a stage where our side hustle actually looks like a viable business we need to start saying no more often.

A member of my VIP coaching Facebook group had an awesome remedy for the "learning how to say no" predicament. She lists the top three priorities she is currently working on and makes decisions based on whether or not they can help her achieve those three things.

So for instance, I've been turning down guest posting opportunities left and right. I've also been updating the blog a whole lot less. Reason being that at the time of writing this book I've got three main priorities: getting this book out into the world by January 2014, preparing my business for a

New Year with a heap load of clients, and getting back into a daily fitness routine.

Updating my blog three times a week (or even once a week) does not accomplish those things. Neither does guest posting on sites that won't really grow my audience.

By learning to say no we can steer clear of what we don't need while focusing on the right things. This applies to business growth, how you spend your money, and even other areas of your life.

LEARNING HOW TO SAY NO EXERCISE

- *What are the three main priorities you are currently working on?*

- *What activities/tasks will help you accomplish these?*

- *What activities/tasks will not help you accomplish these?*

Learning how to say no does take practice. Chances are it will take us a few tries before we don't feel so guilty about turning something down. Once you realize how much less stress you have in your life as a result of saying no it will become a whole lot easier.

Working Based on Energy, Not Schedules

Danielle LaPorte has a brilliant quote on her blog. It says the following:

"When you decide to go after a new dream, you need to give less to your current reality and more to your desired reality. I see this struggle especially with people who want to leave a situation to start their own thing: You set your sights on your dream, and yet, you keep giving your current, kinda-crappy situation 110% — out of habit, obligation, fear or image control. You keep putting in crazy hours at your current thing, while the New Thing just... waits for you to find the time... getting the scraps of your energy and attention.

*And New Thing happens a year later, or
three years later — or never.*

*Take your energy out of what you don't want
to be doing anymore so you can put it what
you really want to be doing."*

Pure freakin' genius.

Remember, our time and energy are
precious. We do not have to spend time
doing things we don't want to do. Is a
project not working? Scrap it. Is that book
not really helping? Stop reading it. Is that
client being a total pain in your ass? Direct
them elsewhere.

If we don't manage our energy we can
waste a lot of time on things that will not
help us achieve our desired reality.

There's another really cool thing about
energy, it can actually help you work more
efficiently. Here's what I mean. When I cut
my day job hours in half to pursue my
business I thought I had to spend my
business days working between the hours of
9:00am and 6:00pm. I failed miserably.

You want to know why? Because I'm
not a morning person. Good heavens I have
tried to be one, but I just don't work well in
the mornings! Instead, I'd rather spend my

mornings meditating, moving my body, making an awesome breakfast and reading positive literature. Then I'm ready to work with no caffeine necessary.

Deadlines are important, set schedules not so much. On average I spend four to six hours a day doing any real work that will move me forward. It may look I'm working 12 hours based on my Facebook statuses, but I'm not. I may also be really enthusiastic one day put in 10 hours, and the next day I'll just take it off entirely. I'm also not dreading my life on those occasional 10 hour days, because when you're doing what you love you often don't notice it's work.

The reason this works well for me is because I work based on my energy levels. I know that I get my best work done in the late morning and early afternoon so that's what I reserve for the heavy lifting!

Granted I can't always have a day when I work five hours in the middle of the day and that's it, but I try my best. On those days when I do have to put in some extra elbow grease because of a looming deadline or client schedules, I make sure to compensate with rest at the next available opportunity.

We're used to cramming in as much work as possible during the day because we treat it with such urgency. This philosophy of being as productive as possible in the shortest amount of time is hurting more than it's helping.

We're also used to hyping ourselves up on caffeine to keep pushing through. This is only a major stressor on the body and the brain - one that in actuality makes you LESS productive.

Don't get me wrong, I'm in no way saying that caffeine is bad. I've been known to love my cup of Joe. What I'm saying is we tend to rely on stimulants to get us through the day as we cram in as much as possible. This only leads to unhealthy habits and puts you on a fast track to burnout.

Your work will be there waiting for you tomorrow when you decide to pick it back up again. Take as many breaks as you need and focus on one or two big things a day. Simple as that.

ENERGY MANAGEMENT EXERCISE

- *When do you feel the most energy throughout the day?*

- *When do you feel the least amount of energy?*

- *What work can you get done during your energy peak?*

- *How can you rest or do something nice for yourself when your energy is low?*

- *What does an ideal work day look like to you?*

Rest is just as important as getting stuff done. If we plow through our days without taking care of ourselves we in actuality become less productive. Start practicing energy management instead of time management and see how it goes!

Building Your A Team

"Listen. Choose the people in your life carefully & surround yourself with artists & experts at their craft....then listen to what they have to say. They're the ones who will help you on the way to the top."

- P. Diddy

One of the biggest concerns I hear from clients is that they don't know where to go for support. They have this incredible idea and their family thinks they are nuts. They have this passion that's driving them into blind ambition and their friends don't get it. They know they are on to something but they feel alone in the process.

They also eventually realize that they can't do everything by themselves - and they shouldn't have to! But instead of turning this into something helpful, they just add more stress onto themselves. It's often times we put an insane amount of pressure on ourselves to find the perfect mentor. I can't even count how many articles I've read on job sites that make finding a mentor seem like awkward dating.

The bad news is that it sucks to feel this way. It really can become lonely to go into business for yourself if you're not making sure to surround yourself with awesome people. Finding a mentor can also prove to be challenging at times, especially if you're so anxious about it.

The good news is that when you're running your own business you choose who to let into your A Team. It's also not as difficult to find mentors or friends in this world. In all honesty I have found that entrepreneurs are some of the most laid back people around.

Thanks to the internet there are a ton of places where you can find these people. From Facebook groups to social networking sites, you can connect with amazing people from all over the world. I've even met some of my greatest colleagues because I commented on their blog years ago.

A couple of my favorite resources for connections with like-minded people include Hungry Entrepreneurs and HerFuture.com. There are, of course, a ton of other kinds of groups on the web and you'll be guided to exactly which ones you need.

You can also start hitting up local groups. Just go to Meetup.com and search what you're looking for.

I want to make it clear that you should have criteria for your A Team. Just like you only want friends you can trust and have a good time with, the same applies for the people who will help you with your business. Make sure they get your vision and make sure they'll help you elevate your very existence, both in terms of business and your personal life.

You must surround yourself with people who are going to take you higher - from your web designer to your colleagues. You want to become friends with people who are in the trenches with you and are on the same page about how to deal with obstacles. You want to find mentors and coaches who will actually take the time to teach you. Lastly, if you want to make more money start hanging out with people who are making it!

Below you'll find an exercise that will help you start building your A Team so you can skyrocket into business success.

BUILDING YOUR A TEAM EXERCISE

1. What characteristics do you want your team members to possess?

2. What value are they going to provide for you and your business? What value can you provide in return? (Remember, it's not all about you!)

3. List 3 people you'd like to reach out to and introduce yourself via email.

Getting clear on the kind of people you want to surround yourself with will not only help your business, it will also enrich your life outside of work. One the fastest ways to make more money is to make sure that your life is filled with richness, building your A Team is a good place to start!

Amanda Abella

Trade in Your To Do List for a Ta Da List

The idea of changing your "To Do" list to a "Ta Da" list has been around for ages. It's the idea that instead of stressing out over everything you have to do you give yourself kudos for everything you've gotten done.

I tried to Google the origin of this terminology and was really upset when I realized that people had turned Ta Da lists back into To Do lists. The name may have been different but the concept was the same: how much can people cram into one day?

Well, I'm bringing it back! Screw your To Do list! Seriously, it really is just another form of stress.

Don't get me wrong, you can use your calendar to organize your priorities in a reasonable manner. However, at the end of the day I want you to list off everything you accomplished.

Figuring Out Your Priorities

Jim Collins, the author of *Good to Great* is famous for his quote on prioritizing, "If you have more than three priorities, you have no priorities."

I challenge you to bring it down to two priorities a day. If you get anything else done then it's considered icing on the already awesome cake.

That's all you really need in a day anyway, two of the most important things that need to get done. If you're not sure or you've got a lot of irons in the fire (as I usually do) look at your calendar and start giving yourself some reasonable deadlines for tasks.

For instance, in addition to writing this book I was still working with coaching clients one-on-one and writing articles for several editors. It was also Holiday season which means lots of social time (yes, fun time is considered a good thing and you should have it often). I had to give myself a reasonable amount of time to actually complete this book and everything that comes with it so I gave myself three months.

Not three days, not three weeks, not three years. Three months. I picked a deadline for the completed project and then proceeded to give myself deadlines for everything it entails including getting a cover designed, editing, formatting for Kindle, formatting for print, and promotion.

This time leeway allowed me to still manage all other aspects of my business while working on a long term project. It also was just close enough to give me the drive I needed to get it done.

Another method that works well for me is figuring out my weekly goals. Every week I make a list of things I would be happy with if they got done. Again, if I get more than that done I consider it gravy.

As you can see, I pick my priorities based on what will make me feel happy and satisfied. Couple that with remembering to stick to activities that will propel you toward getting paid and your work days become less stressful.

CREATING PRIORITIES EXERCISE

What will you be happy with if it gets done this week?

How can you split this up into two priorities a day?

Celebrating Your Ta Da's!

At the end of each day I make a list of what I got done. It is so much nicer to track your accomplishments than it is to list off everything you still need to do. Make it a daily practice, say some gratitude for an awesome work day, and enjoy the rest of your time.

Set Up Accountability Systems

Each morning at 10:00am (Remember, I'm not a morning person!) I am on the phone with my accountability buddy. We go over the previous days accomplishments, list off our two main priorities for the day, and keep each other accountable all day long.

I also have a mastermind/book club on Google Hangouts every Friday with a couple of my closest colleagues. We let off steam, throw ideas around, and hold each other accountable.

And finally, you can bet I have a lot of coaches in my life. Quite frankly, every coach needs and mostly likely has a coach. Even Oprah has coaches! It's like the teachers are also always students.

The point is that I've got a lot of people who will lovingly push me when I need it, hear me out, and tell me to chill out every once in a while. We also make sure to check in with each other all the time.

Since incorporating these systems I've gotten more done than I ever thought possible while still enjoying my life. It took me six months after hiring my own coach to have a viable business. This book came to be because my mastermind group lovingly rooted me on every step of the way. By also implementing a daily accountability call I get more done in a few hours than I ever imagined.

Even during those moments when I have a lot on my plate and looming deadlines I know I'll be able to get what I need done.

Your Personal Life Should Go On Your Calendar Too

I cannot live without Google Calendar. Aside from scheduling my work activities I also use it to schedule everything else. Why? Because your life is just as important as your work.

I will schedule lunch with friends and coffee dates as if they are doctor's appointments I must go to. I block out time to work out and take care of myself. I even put cleaning on the calendar so I make sure it gets done.

In conclusion, you are incredibly valuable as a person, the work you put into the world is worthy of being shared, and your personal time is more valuable than anything else you've got. Once you really begin to realize this work days become a lot easier.

You no longer have to put in 14 hour days 7 days a week to make money. You no longer have to do things you don't want to do. You can make time to take care of yourself. You can get everything you need and more done while still having the time to spend on things that truly matter in life.

If you want to have a viable business with a personal life to match, you must change your mentality toward work. By implementing the strategies in this section you are already well on your way.

PART TWO

DON'T CONVINCE;
CONTRIBUTE!

Don't convince; contribute!

Here's a mistake a ton of entrepreneurs make, especially those who primarily work online: they think they don't have to learn anything about sales.

Sorry to break it to you, but very rarely will someone click through and purchase your service just because you have it posted on your website.

The truth of the matter is that if you expect to survive in business you need to learn a thing or two about sales, connections, and networking. Essentially, you have to learn how to build relationships and persuade people.

This may seem like a bummer but in the long run it's not. So often I hear the following when it comes to money, sales, and service based businesses:

- *Sales is so gross! I hate doing it!*

- *Oh I could NEVER charge that much!*

- *Well I'm really providing a service so I can't charge money - it's icky and wrong.*

- *I'm a really spiritual person so I shouldn't care about making money.*

- *I'm a writer (healer, artist, personal trainer, insert title here) so I'm just going to be poor.*

- *I can't do sales because there is so much competition.*

NEWS FLASH: Those are all a bunch of stories you don't need to buy into. In fact, you literally can't AFFORD to buy into them.

If you think you're going to be poor then yes, you will be poor. If you think all writers are broke, then you will be a broke writer. If you think making a sale is awkward, then you will continue to have awkward sales calls. If you think you need to completely deplete yourself in order to provide a service, you will never make the money you actually want to make. If you think everyone seen as your competition is out to screw you over then that's what you'll see over and over again.

Amanda Abella

It's Okay to Want Money

Let's clarify something here: just because you love something doesn't mean it shouldn't make you any money.

I love coaching. I love writing. I love helping people figure out how to have healthy relationships with work and money. It's fun to me! And you can bet your ass I want to make a lot of money doing it.

Why the hell wouldn't I?

I need to fill my cup so that I can continue serving others. The more money I make the more I can provide for myself and my family. The more money I make the more time I can spend developing products and services that actually help my clients (let's face it, it takes moolah). The more money I make the more I can do things I enjoy, like traveling. The more money I make the more I can donate to my favorite charities.

Last time I checked there is absolutely nothing wrong with providing for your family, giving more value to your clients, making sure you're taken care of, and actually enjoying your life. The truth of the matter is that it takes money to do so, and the way you get this money is by actually selling.

Notice how the words "I want to make money so I can be rich and famous" did not come out of my mouth. The true art of sales isn't about getting rich quick or taking advantage of people. Money, in and of itself, also isn't an evil problem - remember it doesn't actually exist, it's just energy - the misuse and distortion of it is.

Wiping these stories out of your mental hard drive is a good place to start in making the conversations about money and sales way less uncomfortable.

The first step in unraveling the sales drama is to identify what stories we tell ourselves about sales. Maybe sales make you totally uncomfortable. Maybe you've been told your entire life that your line of work will make you poor. Maybe you feel that good sales people have different genetic coding than you do. Maybe you feel like money is dirty and as such you shouldn't ask for it.

Whatever it is, call yourself out on your bullshit right now using the following exercise.

FEELINGS ABOUT SALES EXERCISE

What stories have you told yourself about sales?

What makes you think it's awkward or uncomfortable?

We are the only ones who give sales any meaning, not the other way around. Essentially, sales aren't awkward because of their nature, in reality we're the ones being awkward!

When we identify what we are so afraid of it starts to lose its power over us. We can also actively work to change it. In the next few pages we'll start doing just that!

Practicing Your New Sales Mentality

I had one client who totally nailed it when it came to shifting her mindset around sales. She was a former recruiter for a big time European company and totally hated selling for her own business. It made her feel gross and uncomfortable even though she knew she was providing something valuable for people.

Through our work together we discovered some connections between her old job as a recruiter and her new career as an entrepreneur. When she was a recruiter she would essentially persuade people to take a job, which is already a form of sales. These people benefited from her persuasion because their jobs would allow them to support themselves and their families.

By applying that idea to her current business she was able to come up with the mantra "Recruiting Ideal Clients is Fun." This totally shifted the way she did business - from pitching and closing sales to creating products and finding partners! The uncomfortable feelings subsided and eventually disappeared as she realized that closing sales for her business is the same concept as recruiting the ideal people for a job.

At the end of the day sales doesn't have to be complicated or stressful. By owning the fact that you actually want to make money, and being okay with it, you can open the door to all of the abundance around you. Then you can worry about putting sales funnels, referrals, and pitches into place.

Just remember these two things:

• You must make sure you are taken care of if you are to continue serving others.

• It's all about working with the right people and providing them with value.

Why Do You Want The Money?

One thing clients have found really helpful when getting more comfortable around the idea of asking for money is to identify why they want it to begin with.

Like I mentioned before, there is nothing wrong with wanting things and wanting things takes money. Money, essentially, just allows to do stuff.

So what is it that you want to do? Do you want to put money into a retirement account so you can have something for the golden years? Do you want to fill up your emergency fund? Do you need to pay off some debt? Do you want to take a sweet vacation?

There really are no wrong answers, though something that can help you narrow it down for yourself is to identify what you actually value.

We dabbled in this in Part One with the example about the $500 shoes. Now instead of figuring out what value you provide for clients, we're going to figure out what you value as an individual. This will help you figure out why you want the money you are asking for. It will also help you figure out what you should and should not be spending money on. Bottom line, we're killing two birds with one stone.

WHAT DO YOU VALUE? EXERCISE

Take out your last bank statement and look at your expenses. Take out a pen and put a dot next to the expenses that made you feel like shit when you purchased them. Then take out a highlighter (preferably a bright, happy color) and mark the expenses that you actually enjoyed spending the money on.

Then, answer the following questions:

What expenses made you feel crappy?

When did you feel better about spending money?

What do you enjoy doing?

What do you enjoy spending money on?

When I did this exercise myself I came to notice that when I spend $200 bucks on clothes then I don't feel so great the next day. Simply put, I don't value clothing that much. So I stopped binging on sweaters so I could put the money toward things I actually value like travel and growing my business. I could spend twice that much money on conferences and I won't mind paying off the credit card because I'm okay with spending to grow my business.

This exercise also helped you identify why you want the money you're asking people for. Rather than it being some abstract concept, now you have a reason to feel like you deserve to get paid.

Mind Shift: It's Not Sales, It's Sharing

Now that we've addressed that it's okay to want money and we know why you want it we can get down and dirty with the process of asking for money.

Sales is oftentimes seen as a do-or-die shark tank of incessant competition to make a quick buck.

We feel awkward, put on the spot, and hate asking people to buy our stuff.

However, when selling is done properly nothing could be further from the truth -

especially when it comes to small businesses.

What if I told you sales wasn't actually as icky as most people make it out to be? What if I told you it's not even really sales, it's sharing?

You have a product or service that can help a certain person. When you find this person you build a relationship and share something that can help them. That's it!

Done correctly it's not awkward because you're going to the right places, talking to the right people, and sharing information that can help them. It's not hard balling, it's not being pushy, and it's not roping your friends into trying to help you to sell to anyone who will purchase something from you.

Picture this: Have you ever been to a really awkward Mary Kay party? Or Avon? Or candles? Or Tupperware?

You know what I'm talking about. A party where everyone the representative knew was invited, Facebook posts were published, emails were sent, and you yourself are probably there as a favor.

Why is it so painful? Because the representative is trying to sell products to people who probably don't really want them or have a need for them. So they sweat. They fumble through a sales pitch and all you really want to do is get out of there and grab a beer.

This isn't to say that all sales reps are making this mistake (Hey! We've all seen the pink Mary Kay cars!). What it does show is the key difference between a successful sales rep and one who struggles to move the product.

Rather than sharing information with people who needed or wanted it, that rep was trying to push a product on people who didn't even have a need for it; thus making it very awkward.

Now imagine only talking to people you want to work with. Imagine establishing relationships so even if they don't come on as a client now they probably will later (and often times do). Imagine what it's like to share relevant and helpful information to people you know you can serve.

Different vibe, right?

You see, you probably wouldn't want to work with everyone who comes your way anyway. In fact, I can guarantee that you don't.

Think about it: let's say you run a coaching business for women wanting to move up the corporate ladder. Are you going to work with stay-at-home moms? Probably not.

What you want to do, and what smart entrepreneurs do, is work with the *right* people. This is a major key in creating your sacred business - knowing who you can help and who you will allow into your sacred space. Not only will it make your work more enjoyable, but you'll actually get paid to have fun.

You've probably heard the term target market. And you've probably stressed yourself out trying to figure out just who your target market is. Maybe you have a fuzzy idea of who you want to work with and maybe you've got seven.

That's all a very good start. And I will walk you through the rest. By the end of this section you'll see sales in a whole new way.

Who Are You Serving?

So many entrepreneurs have no idea who they serve, despite the fact that every single book on sales and marketing attempts to help you figure it out.

If you're reading this book chances are you have a fuzzy idea but no clear picture. Or maybe your picture is kind of clear but something is missing.

I could go on forever about how to figure out your target market. For instance, in my own business I've come to notice that I create products and services based on struggles I have faced in my own life. I also work really well with women who are very much like me. (Not a shocker since like attracts like).

I can tell you where these people hang out, what they're employment history looks like, the kinds of businesses they would like to have, and what they value in life. I can also tell you what they struggle with.

How did I figure this out?

By actually coaching people! I took my fuzzy idea of wanting to be a career coach and put it to the test. I started telling everyone I knew I was coaching people with their careers and started taking calls. I also set up coffee dates just to pick their brains - starting with my friends who had expressed interest.

The more I coached the more I realized common themes:

1. I really dig creative entrepreneurial spirits. In fact I do some of my best work with them.

2. Most of my clients have worked regular jobs in the past - and they've been awesome at them!

3. Most want a business for the same basic reasons: flexibility, freedom, fun, and to be of service to some greater good. The specifics may vary

but it can basically be summed up in those words.

4. I do my best work with incredibly ambitious, positive, and healthy people.

5. Age isn't really a factor with my ideal client, but mindset is. You can be 29, 39, or 49 and it wouldn't matter so long as we're on the same page about mindset.

6. Most of my clients have some sort of spirituality in their lives - some are more woo woo than others but they can all get down with it.

7. They all had the same struggles: dealing with money, quitting crappy situations that aren't serving them, building a business that is authentic to them, learning how to maneuver blogging for business, and becoming an employee of their business with a sprinkle of needing a confidence boost.

There's a heady sales term for this you'll probably recognize: market research.

So if you're still kind of fuzzy on who you are serving I want you to do a couple of things.

First, come up with a way to make market research fun. Maybe you start going to funky events, maybe you start with the people closest to you, maybe you offer free calls to people on a social networking site you dig, maybe you put on a speaking event (gasp!).

I had one client who simply sent out a nice email asking to pick people's brains over coffee or Skype. So simple yet so effective! Within 30 minutes she had two meetings already confirmed. Here's her template. I've broken it down for you so you can see why it worked.

You'll find the email script below with important descriptions in bold.

Hi [name],

As you know I'm in the process of getting my personal training business up and running. [letting people know what she's up to] Throughout my life I've faced a lot of challenges that sprung from my lack of self-confidence. This affected me in different areas of my life - from careers to relationships. Fortunately I was able to overcome them with a support system of fitness and self-awareness. [quick backstory to her business and how she plans on helping people]

Meeting with you will help me figure out how to incorporate this system in order to better serve my clients, find out what specific areas I should focus on with them, and develop an effective package that will help them overcome the same barriers I once had. **[Making them a part of the process]** *In exchange for your time I can offer* **[free session, consultation, discount, etc.] [incentive]**

You can use my scheduling tool to pick a time to chat (so much easier than emailing back and forth): **[link] [make it easy for them!]**

For your convenience we can also meet **[in person, Skype, on the phone, other option] [flexibility that works for you and them]**

Thank you in advance for meeting with me! I know that your insights will help me develop a great program for my clients! **[Thanking them and including them.]**

Once you've been collecting data from people start noticing patterns. What are they struggling with? How and when are you best serving them? What are the similarities between all these people? When do you feel excited and ready to work?

Before you know it you'll have a much better picture of who you work best with and how you can solve their problems.

What if I know who I'm meant to serve?

Great! But that doesn't mean you should stop talking to people, picking brains, or refining your ideal client. That's how you can come up with new products or services that will help them out.

In continuously asking for feedback and talking to people I found out there was a serious need for a book like this one. Never stop inquiring. And certainly never stop listening.

Amanda Abella

Selling from a Place of Service

Here's the really cool thing about my client's method of using coffee dates for market research - she scored her first paying client at one of these meetings!

It wasn't awkward, it wasn't scary, and she didn't push a sale - all she did was come from a genuine place of service and ask "How can I help you?" during a simple conversation about her upcoming business and health related topics.

The person she was talking to needed a trainer who was well versed in the area of stress reduction. Long story short, she made a sale right then and there.

The art of conversation is key when making sales. Again, this isn't about hard balling or pounding someone into submission until they buy your services. It's about sharing helpful information with someone who actually needs it and then asking them for their business.

It's about trading value for value - and there is nothing weird, scammy, or uncomfortable about that.

Late last year I went to the Florida Yoga Journal Conference where I saw Marianne Williamson give a keynote. It was all about work, money, service, and politics - and it was absolutely brilliant!

She was very adamant about the fact that there is absolutely nothing wrong with capitalism, money, or asking for money. There is nothing wrong with trading fair value for value. Let's face it; capitalism has been good to those of us living in first world countries.

The problem is when capitalism and money lose their ethical center. So for instance, if you're trying to sell someone on a product or service they really don't need because all you want to do is make more money, you're scamming them. That is not a fair trade of value which just leads to problems.

Amanda Abella

One of two things will happen: either you're going to have a very hard time making sales or even if you make the sale you're going to feel incredibly crummy.

Meanwhile, if you're clear about who you're serving and what problems you're fixing for them you can come from a place of service and simply have a natural conversation with prospective clients. Not everyone will come on and pay you, but it's going to be a lot easier to make the money you need (and more!) if you come from a place of actually helping people fix their problems.

People can smell BS from a mile away. They know when they are being scammed or coerced into buying something. They can also smell desperation.

The best thing you can do is start coming from a place of service and practice the idea of trading value for value. Coming from this perspective makes the whole process a lot easier. If you have an energy of serving instead of "I need to make this sale so I can pay my rent!" you'll be much more likely to close sales.

The Pearly White Gates of Your Sacred Business

In *Book Yourself Solid*, Michael Port talks about his velvet rope policy for his business. Essentially, this is where you evaluate whether or not a prospective client is a good fit for you. If they are then you invite them to your services.

Since I like to teach clients that their businesses are totally sacred and full of value I like to switch up the words a bit. In my world it's not just a velvet rope, it's the Pearly White Gates where I make sure you can enter my sacred space. Just like St. Peter is said to be the gate keeper of heaven, I teach my clients that they are the gate keepers of their businesses.

What do I mean by this? Well, once you have figured out who you want to work with you just can't let *anybody* into your world.

What you need a system in place so a) you get people inquiring about your services and b) you know whether or not you can and want to work with them. Trust me, this will save you oodles of headaches down the road.

Here's an example of what I mean. For me, my Pearly White Gate is the **Fire Up Your Biz** promotion. It's a free 30 minute laser coaching session where I help people formulate their next business and/or money steps. By the end of it I can discern whether or not I can coach them.

If the answer is yes, I **invite** them to come on as a private coaching client (key word being invite. Remember, you're sharing not selling.) If the answer is no I either refer them to someone who can help them, direct them to a blog post, or invite them to join a Facebook group of blog readers.

That same client who sent out those emails to conduct market research was able to come up with an offering based on what her market was telling her. She called it

Make Money Your Honey

Trilogy and tailored a free 30 minute Mind-Body-Soul warm up to meet potential clients, give them a taste of the program, and discern whether or not they were a good fit.

PEARLY WHITE GATES EXERCISE

What is your Pearly White Gate?

What value do you provide for your idea client in the Pearly White Gates stage?

How can you make it more efficient?

If you don't have a Pearly White Gate how can you create one?

Getting People to Your Pearly White Gate

Similar to your services, people aren't just going to automatically sign up for your Pearly White Gate - some might, but chances are you need to actually tell people about it!

Here's my approach: If someone connects with me on Twitter or my Facebook page, I shoot them an email. If someone comments on my blog, I email them. I occasionally email subscribers with promotion updates. I announce it on Facebook and Twitter. I invite people in person at networking events and functions. I also rely heavily on referrals (More on that later. It merits its own section.)

This may seem really overwhelming but it's not. The only thing you have to remember is to ask people to take you up on the free promotion. Not everyone will say yes, but the majority probably will. Soon it becomes second nature and you learn how to bring it up in conversation.

Referrals

My coach and mentor Jennie Mustafa-Julock taught me some of the best business practices I use over and over again. One of these techniques is to ask for referrals. Seriously, she's like the Queen of Referrals. No joke.

It's simple, really. If you've already got clients ask them to send people your way. Chances are they hang out with people similar to them. You can also hit up LinkedIn (goldmine!), Facebook, Twitter, past prospective clients, and networking events.

I even go as far as asking people who aren't necessarily my ideal clients to send people over. After all, just because they aren't my kind of client doesn't mean they don't know people who are.

The point is it's a lot easier to have other people do your selling for you. Before you know it you have an army of people keeping an eye out for you. Here are some of my favorite ways to use referrals:

Current Clients: I often ask my clients that if they find anyone that will dig my coaching to send them over my way. There's no better advocate than your own clients!

LinkedIn: I sent out a message on LinkedIn that let people know about my Fire Up My Biz promotion and what kind of people I was looking to help. Not only did I get referrals, I got people asking to take me up on my offer directly!

Email Subscribers: I sent the same message I used for LinkedIn to my email subscribers. Because I was so specific about who I was looking for many of my subscribers signed up themselves!

Colleagues: I have a list of people I can refer in case I decide I can't work with someone. These people are well aware of it. Since I scratch their back with referrals, they scratch mine.

Facebook Groups: I'm a part of several Facebook groups for entrepreneurs and coaches. I find them much more effective in getting people to help you out than Facebook pages.

What I've created is a referral machine where people know what I'm looking for as well as what I'm offering thus making the sales process a whole lot easier.

Making Referrals Easy

One very important aspect about the referral process is to make it as easy as possible for people to help you out. People may want to really help you, but let's face it; life totally gets in the way. As a result you kind of have to hold their hands on the follow through.

I use Tweetables all they have to do is click on. I also basically wrote an intro email for them so all they have to do is copy, paste, and send to their friends.

Super easy! Super convenient!

Clearing Space within Your Sacred Business

This step may hurt at first, but I promise it's super liberating! Now that you're talking to people through your market research, have your Pearly White Gates set up, and have created a referral system it's time to make room for all the people coming your way!

How do you do that? By dumping your dud clients. You know exactly who they are. The ones that are more trouble than they are worth. The ones you don't really enjoy working with. Or, the ones that you believe may be better served by someone else.

Remember your business is sacred and if you're not actually enjoying working with these people then you can't provide your best work anyway.

Be unapologetic, but don't be an asshole about it either. Simply refer them to someone who will better be able to serve them. That way you still look good and they may even send you referrals.

You'll also want to shelf any projects that are not currently serving your market. Don't worry, you can always modify them or pick them back up again later (much like I did with this book) - it's just that now may not be the right time for them as you make space for your ideal clients to come in. These clients will then let you know what they need so you can create projects that will benefit them.

If you need a refresher on how to decide which projects to take on and which ones you should put away head back to How to Start Providing Value for Your Business.

The Sprinkles on Top

The Sprinkles on Top are what I like to call the extra offerings that not only help current and prospective clients; they also help you run your business smoother. I'll walk you through my sprinkles so you see what I mean.

Facebook Groups

I have two Facebook groups associated with my business. The first is for VIPs. That means these are where my paying clients go for extra support during our time together. They have resources to other coaches and materials, and above all they can connect with other like-minded individuals. I know everyone in this group on a personal level. It's certainly a favorite of clients and offers them exclusivity when coaching with me.

The second is my Ambassadors group. This is for people who have expressed explicit interest in helping me grow and promote my business. This is also where I send prospective clients that may not be a good fit right now. Why? Because not everyone who isn't a good fit is a bad prospective client. It could just be bad timing or that they aren't yet ready for a coach. If that's the case then the Facebook group does several things: first, I've got all these people in one place. Second, I continue having a relationship with them so they don't forget about me. And lastly, I can just follow up with them about coaching when the timing is right.

Email Coaching

My private clients have unlimited email coaching with me for the duration of our time together. Just because we're not on the phone doesn't mean we can't get coached!

The point here is to provide exclusivity for your top notch clients while still connecting with those who may not be ready for your services yet. It's so easy to get on Facebook and create a group and it literally costs nothing. I've known others who use email lists or have some free event once a month like a Google Hangout.

Competition is Dead

In October of 2013 I flew to St. Louis to give my first big talk at The Financial Blogger Conference. My talk was entitled *Competition is Dead: How to Have a Rockstar Blog by Sharing, Collaborating, and Working With Your Competitors*.

The premise was simple: rather than griping, clawing, and thinking that there are limited resources why don't we all just do our thing and help each other out? This may seem naive, again, because this is in complete contrast to what we've been taught about competition.

We're taught that competition is scary and intense. We're taught that we must step on people. We're especially taught that there is a limited amount of money going around.

We saw this on a larger scale with the global economy and it obviously didn't work. If it did the economy wouldn't have tanked and millions wouldn't have lost their jobs. So what makes you think it will work for your own business?

Fortunately, the days of incessant competition are quickly diminishing because we're coming to realize that it doesn't benefit anyone. Bloggers and entrepreneurs are often times at the forefront of a collaborative economy that focuses on helping each other out. If you feel like you need help, guidance, or even a swift kick in the pants reach out to others for their input.

A negative form of competition also leads us to try and re-invent the wheel and make things more difficult for ourselves because we need to be "unique" and "different." We put a lot of stress and effort into being the first ones to ever do something. In reality this is impossible.

We all know that there is nothing new under the sun. Besides, what makes your business unique and different is you! No one has your same story! There's your angle!

Furthermore, if you come up with something "too different" then no one will have any idea what you are trying to sell. If something has been proven to work and you are good at it, go for it! There really is no need to make it more difficult for yourself.

In terms of branding, angles, copy, unique voices, and what makes you different than the next guy - you'll figure it all out organically as you go along. Start with your own story in relation to what you are offering and take it from there.

Finally, competition negatively affects us in so far is it sometimes makes us feel inadequate. We give up on pursuing what we want because we think someone else is doing it better, and as a result there isn't enough left for us.

In my talk I used the example of Pat Flynn of *Smart Passive Income* fame. There are plenty of people out there who can teach you a thing or two about making passive income. Just because Pat Flynn may have done it first (and he probably didn't actually come up with it first) doesn't mean that everyone else should sit down and keep their mouths shut.

I once had a client who was debating whether or not to quit her job and pursue her own endeavors. She had a passion for helping women become financially independent and wanted to teach women how to manage their careers. She was also great at making money. During one of our sessions she said "I really want to do this, but Suze Orman is already doing it! Why would anyone listen to me?"

At this point I responded with, "Because Suze Orman is going to die one day." I didn't mean to be so morbid (fortunately my client found it funny), but I did make a very good point.

We always need new blood to come up and teach others. It's a natural cycle of life. Those who came before us pass on and we'll need someone else to take their place. Besides, I happen to think Suze Orman would agree with me on this one.

This client proceeded to resign from her position as a VP of marketing for a tech start-up to pursue who own endeavors. A couple of weeks later she was speaking at Google.

Do not hide your gifts just because you think someone out there is already doing it. We need new voices. We need people to share their stories with the world. There is also more than enough money, clients, and readers to go around and those who are truly successful know this on a visceral level.

PART THREE:

MONEY: FROM "OH SHIT!" TO "I GOT THIS!"

Amanda Abella

Money: From "Oh Shit!" to "I Got This"

What's the number one fear people have about going into business for themselves? It overshadows a fear of self-promotion, time management, and failure - though it's definitely the root fear of all three.

MONEY.

We've been addressing different aspects of common money stories throughout the book, but now it's time for the heavy lifting.

(Hey, I had to ease you into it!)

I'm going to be honest with you - this is probably one of the biggest mental shifts that takes the most practice.

That's totally okay though, because this will be like working out a muscle. One day at a time you'll get stronger and become more confident in your ability to make money for the long haul.

How do I know this? Because it wasn't until I made this significant shift around my finances that consistent dollars started coming in the door.

Quite frankly, a part of me didn't think I could pull it off so I was obviously blocking money from coming in. Once I identified common money myths, got clear on my money story (and where it came from), took an unapologetic inventory of my finances, and brought on new beliefs about money things started to change at a rapid pace.

I started landing coaching clients. I got writing offers. I kept finding commission sale notifications in my inbox. Awesome opportunities presented themselves to me and the only real change was my mental attitude toward money.

I'm going to be totally honest here: you can do all the work in the world, but unless you believe you deserve to be getting money your bank account is going to be lonely and you're going to struggle. I, myself, had most of the "outside" business stuff in place and still didn't feel comfortable enough to quit my job. Once I started making shifts about money the game totally changed. By month three of working for myself full-time I was making more money than I'd ever made at a regular job.

You also cannot create the kind of work you love with a life to match without looking at your money. You can't just sock your bank account away in a corner and wish for things to magically fix themselves or pretend they don't affect you - you have to take an active part in caring for it and as such caring for yourself.

So let's take our money muscles on a ride.

Debunking Common Money Stories

Chances are you've heard one or all of the following beliefs at some point during your entrepreneurial journey. Allow me to completely debunk them for you.

1. *Entrepreneurship isn't as solid as a stable job.*

I worked in recruiting for some time so I heard this all the time. "Regular jobs are more stable and entrepreneurship is hard." Real talk: job security doesn't actually exist. Millions got laid off during the height of the Great Recession. New management can come in and wipe everyone out. Mergers usually result in lost jobs and maybe your boss is having a crappy day and decided to give you a pink slip.

I'm not so sure what's so secure about leaving your job in someone else's hands. I don't say this to scare you, I just say this so you realize that the only one who can have control over your work and your money is you - and that is pretty damn empowering!

2. *Entrepreneurs are poor.*

Let's clarify: entrepreneurs who don't know what they are doing, who they are serving, and why are poor. People who are looking to make a quick buck are also usually poor. The term poor is also relative depending on how you want to live and that goes back to what you value.

3. *You can move up and make more money in a regular job.*

Right. And while that employee is waiting months for a company to maybe approve an extra 25 cents an hour, entrepreneurs just need to put in a little extra elbow grease or raise their rates whenever they feel they need a bonus.

4. *You get health insurance at a regular job.*

First of all, this isn't necessarily true (I didn't have insurance at a regular job).

Second, many times even at a regular job you're still paying for insurance in some way, shape, or form. Third, there are a ton of options for self-employed individuals and since more people are jumping ship to do their own thing it's definitely a topic on the table.

Is our health insurance situation perfect? Of course not! It never will be. The point here is that you have more options than you think.

5. *I need a 401k.*

Do you need to save for retirement? Absolutely. Do you need a 401k? Not necessarily. Again, not all companies offer this and fewer companies are offering a match - meaning it's coming from your pocket anyway. There are a multitude of different ways to save for retirement, including (but not limited to) lifecycle funds, Roth IRAs and more. Many of which give you more flexibility than a company 401k plan where your employer chooses where your money goes. Oh and get this - you can start with as little as $100 a month!

6. *Taxes are a bitch.*

Okay yeah, taxes are a bitch. But when *aren't* they a bitch? Besides you have a lot of resources, help, and get this - deductions!

What you need to do is absolutely 100% make sure that you are recording how much money you've got coming in and how many business expenses you have. There are a ton of accounting websites to help you with this like Wave and Outright.com. You can also use QuickBooks, Quicken and lots of other software. Or, you can use a good old fashioned accounts receivable spreadsheet and a running list of deductions.

Like I mentioned earlier, I don't say any of this to scare you. I say this so that you realize you have more choices, options, and control over your finances and your work life than you may have been led to believe.

Now that that's out of the way, we can go deeper and focus on what your own personal money story.

What's Your Money Story?

When it comes to money everyone has an opinion, and it would seem that those opinions affect our own beliefs and ideas about money.

For example, we definitely get a lot of our money shit from our parents. We picked up their stories as kids and many times find ourselves sounding like them in our adulthood.

The news doesn't help much either. With incessant deafening stories about unemployment, how broke we are, national debt, lay-offs, banks, mortgages, and on and on and on.

Real talk: it's just a story.

Is the economy in a shit hole? Yeah. Did our parents have a reason to freak out about money? Probably. But there are plenty of people who grew up with the same stories and in the same economy who are thriving more than ever.

Why?

Because they changed their money story.

So what's your money story? Where did it come from? What are you constantly saying about money?

Get really honest here. The sooner we own it the sooner we can start to heal it. Here are some examples:

Money doesn't grow on trees.

There's no money in this economy.

I can't afford that.

I can't make money doing what I love.

Money is the root of all evil.

People who make a lot of money are greedy.

Use the exercise below to get very clear on your money story and where it comes from. Fight the urge to hold back. Pour your heart out on paper and see where it goes.

Remember, no one ever even has to see this so feel free to get up close and personal with your financial story.

MONEY STORY EXERCISE:

Write out your money story.

What have you been telling yourself about your financial situation?

What have you been telling yourself about your business?

Where did these stories come from and how have they affected your finances and business?

What are some of your hidden fears about money?

How has your money story evolved over time?

After you've written it down read it over and find where your mind went into crazy town. When it comes to money we can easily go from "I have credit card debt" to "I'm going to live under a bridge!" in two seconds flat.

Like most people, I got mixed messages about money my entire life. On the one hand I never went without. I lived in a very nice area of Miami, both my parents made good money, they paid for my private college education, and they never really did anything stupid with it. When the Recession changed the game for recent college grads they welcomed me back home with arms wide open. Seriously, they've always been awesome.

But at the same time, I grew up with my parents always complaining about their work situations and how awful it was. Having one parent who worked for the local government and another who worked for big corporations, you can imagine the stories I was hearing from both ends. As a result I grew up thinking that making money had to be hard and may have involved selling your soul.

When I graduated during the Recession money fears were hitting me square in the forehead, and not just me but the entire nation! Think about it, everything we'd been told while growing up - go to school so you can get a good job - went up in smoke. The media further perpetuated this for everyone, but had a particular obsession with detailing the money woes of my generation. Obviously, this affected me greatly and resulted in panic attacks in my early twenties.

I've also had money hang ups in more subtle ways. As much as I hate to admit this somewhere deep in my bones there lives a

Prince Charming complex. Not necessarily that a strapping young and rich man will whisk me away and take care of me financially, but that someone will (be it my family, the government, a boss, or something else).

And the most laughable and subtle money hang up of all - I thought I wouldn't be liked by the opposite sex if I ran my own business and made a lot of money. I thought that I would somehow emasculate them if I did. Talk about sneaky ego stories!

The reason I share the bad, ugly and embarrassing stories I've created around the idea of money is to encourage you all to get honest with yourselves. Go deep with yourself and get it all out, even if you're not sure where the story is coming from!

Look, that Prince Charming complex and the whole "emasculating men" story came out of nowhere for me, and I'm not even sure where they originated. I wrote those out on the page and I was completely shocked and embarrassed, but there was something completely amazing about calling myself out on it. It was as if the subtle yet very strong hold they'd had on me for so long started to weaken.

Don't judge yourself for getting worked up about money, just laugh at it and move on. Because here's the thing, whatever stories you may have picked up about money - whether from your parents, your partners, your broke friends, or society as a whole - do not need to be your story.

You can rewrite your money story any time you want.

Honoring Your Money Story

Now that you've got your money story I want you to take a good hard look at it and come up with a few reasons why you're thankful for it.

Hear me out: Sure, our money stories may make our skin crawl, but as Iyanla Vanzant puts it, sometimes we humans only learn by pain.

How many times have you come up stronger than ever before after a tough time? I'm sure you can think of a few instances from your life and there's no reason money should be any different.

Let's face it, if it wasn't for the hard times we may not be where we are. We may not be ready, willing, and able to make significant changes to our lives.

For example, I could have easily sat and complained about how the Recession ruined my life and then done absolutely nothing about it. That's easy - it's also what keeps you stuck.

So flip the story. Why are you thankful for your money uglies?

Here's my take:

If it wasn't for the Recession I wouldn't have even thought about running my own business. I would have maybe gotten some regular old desk job and stayed there. I wouldn't be teaching clients how to create authentic businesses they love. I wouldn't be teaching audiences at conferences. I wouldn't be doing things I absolutely love and getting paid for them. I wouldn't have written this book!

Sure, maybe I would have had a few less anxiety attacks. Maybe I wouldn't have gotten so depressed for a while there. Maybe I wouldn't have had to struggle as much. But you know what? All of the perceived failures and uncomfortable emotions were worth it, because at the end of the day they kicked my tail into high gear to proclaim what I wanted and then go after it. As I mentioned in the beginning of this book, my past struggles cracked me open so something beautiful could come out.

So what about your money story makes you grateful? Did getting into debt teach you how to manage your money better? Did losing your job give you the opportunity to explore what you love? Did your stint of being unemployed allow you to be there for your child when they needed you most? Did mom and dad's version of money help you realize you didn't want to live the same way?

Dish it out on paper. And remember, even in the darkest of times you can shed a light on it. Once you shine that light the darkness scatters.

Amanda Abella

Become Willing to See Money Differently

Look, I get it, money has a really strong emotional hold on us. Whether we think our value comes from how much money we make or are still reliving childhood stories from not getting what we wanted for Christmas - the ego is a sneaky bitch when it comes to money.

Admittedly, I still sometimes get stuck in my money stories. I'll get a little nervous if I'm putting a big purchase on the credit card (even if I've got the money sitting in the bank). I still sometimes worry that I won't make enough money, despite the fact that I've been making more than ever since venturing out on my own.

When those moments happen it's important to notice them and become willing to see the situation differently. It sounds totally corny and hokey, but hear me out. Think about people who are so stubborn and dead set on their point of view that they can't even see solutions right in front of them. Think about people who complain all the time and as a result never help themselves. It all goes back to that willingness to see things differently; once we're open to a new point of view we can get some answers.

That's all you really need - an open mind and some willingness to see your financial story with a new pair of eyes.

Here's how willingness manifested in my own life. When I was flat broke and couldn't find a job in a horrendous economy I started looking into the possibility of freelance writing. That led to a little blog called Grad Meets World where I started chronicling my adventures of adulthood and shaping my views about work and money.

That blog was my major message that I was not going to be bogged down by statistics and I was going to figure stuff out. Six months later I had a job in career consulting and recruiting for Fortune 500 companies - totally not planned at all even though I was basically writing a career blog.

A little over two years later I was running my own business full time - of which the foundation came from that very same blog. Oh, and I still write to make money and I doubt that's ever going to change.

A coaching client of mine had a similar story. An injury caused her to take some time off from work. During her downtime she started a blog all about money saving tips. Before she knew it people were approaching her for partnerships and freelance work.

A little willingness to see things differently can go a very long way.

When I went into business for myself it required a major shift about the way I saw money. Quite frankly I didn't have time to get bogged down by my bank account or obsess over where money was going to come from. I found that method actually hindered me from making money.

Instead I became willing to learn about money as a means of abundance. I took every money mishap and asked myself "Okay, what's the lesson here? What am I not seeing? Where can I find information that will help me improve this situation?"

Make Money Your Honey

Asking myself these questions has been incredibly helpful because admittedly I don't know the answer to everything (and I suggest you run like the wind if you find anyone who claims they do). For instance, I wanted to invest but needed to educate myself on how to do so. I wanted to pay down credit card debt, but needed to educate myself on making better sales. I'm sure there will be other situations down the road - buying a house for instance - where I will need to reevaluate, research, and learn.

I needed to start trusting that I could figure it out. I needed to trust that I was more than capable of managing whatever money came in. I needed to stop seeing money as a root of all problems and instead take some personal responsibility. Above all, I needed to trust that if I had the right intentions and remained open minded that I would be provided for so I could continue serving the people who need it.

I don't mean this in a hokey new-age way - I mean it in the most practical way possible. Because if I'm stuck in a mental shit storm over my finances then I can't possibly figure out what needs to get done in order for me to thrive.

Furthermore, if I don't know how to manage money then that's going to negatively affect me no matter how much I make or where it's coming from.

They key I had to learn was that it wasn't necessarily all about how much money I could make - it was about making whatever money came in work for me instead of against me.

So every day I said a prayer, I had affirmations all over my computer, and I built my trust muscle through meditation. I did whatever worked to make me more open to finding creative solutions for generating income and managing my finances.

And you know what? It worked. When I really started working with this kind of mentality I had a new good paying writing client within 3 days. When I really walked my talk I quit my job and had 2 additional coaching clients within a week - both of which kept coaching month after month and have brought me even more clients.

By simply trusting the process and saying yes to the steps presented in front of me I was able to create my dream business that provided enough for me to sustain myself at this stage in my life. I realized it wasn't about making quick bucks and it certainly isn't all about the money, but that managing my finances was a way of taking care of myself so that I could serve others.

We'll get more into exactly how I
manage money a little later, but first we
need to address self-worth, because without
it you won't ever rock your net worth.

Rock Your Self-Worth

One of my heroes Gabrielle Bernstein talks about how self-worth affects your net worth. Simply put, if you don't feel like you deserve to be making money, you probably won't.

I know I'm beating a dead horse here, but there's a very good reason for it: it is far too often that we low ball ourselves, think we can't handle a situation, or think we can't make more money.

You can do whatever the hell you want in this life, you just have to believe it and act accordingly.

You need to believe you actually deserve to be making this money. Half of it comes from experience and practice - closing sales, perfecting the pitch, knowing who you're talking to, etc. - which you're getting a lot of already. And the more you put yourself out there the more practice you'll get.

The other half, and truthfully the real basis of being successful in any area of your life, has nothing to do with money - it has to do with trusting yourself.

You need to become your own biggest fan in the money and business department. You need to believe you actually deserve this and can handle cracking open the bank account - and I'm positive that in some way, shape, or form you already believe it because you purchased this book.

Now we need to rev that up and make you feel unstoppable! The following exercise will help you see where you've rocked it in the finance department. It will also help you take personal responsibility about your current money pickle.

ROCK YOUR SELF-WORTH EXERCISE

Answer the following questions.

1. Where can you sing your own praises in the money department?

2. *What money issues do you need to resolve? What was your part in creating them?*

3. *What are you ALREADY doing to resolve these issues? (This can be something as simple as paying more than the minimum on your last credit card balance.)*

4. *What steps have you already taken to manage your finances?*

By admitting where we goofed up it loses its power over us. We're not playing games. We're not covering things up. We're simply admitting that we're human and there is major liberation in that.

Similarly, by singing our own praises and acknowledging even the smallest wins we rev up that part of us that can come up with solutions.

Daily mental shifts: the practical, the fun, and the seemingly crazy

It can be really hard to go from a lack mentality to one of abundance. And it can be really hard to think you're worthy on those days when things aren't going so smoothly. It's really like a muscle you have to keep working out. Day by day you get stronger and more confident about your abilities to bring in that income.

Fortunately, there are a ton of tools you can use to deal with this. You'll find some of my favorite methods below. You should make it as easy as possible to reach for your funny money busting tools while undergoing these mental shifts.

If you have to cover your room in affirmations, do it. If physical activity works best for you make it easy to do it (I had one client who would hang weighted jump ropes on her door knob so it would be the first thing she sees when she gets home.) Phone reminders, putting it in your planner, sending yourself an email, whatever works!

Affirmations

Affirmations are a great way to separate yourself from your mental money shit storm. I have a post-it on my laptop that says the following:

I believe in creative possibilities for abundance.

I see thoughts of lack as an opportunity for financial learning.

I believe I am worthy of what I ask for.

Every time I'm having a bad day, freaking out about money, or my bills make me nervous I recite those affirmations as a reminder that I'm working on shifting these ideas in my business and my life.

I may not feel all zenned out right away, but it does allow me to at least snap out of the money fear spiral.

I also have these affirmations on my Google Calendar and on my phone - because

I am THAT serious about not being bogged down by money.

Meditation and Breath Work

I love meditation and breath work. Nothing brings you back to center quite like taking some very deep breaths and clearing your mind of whatever you've got going on.

It's a common misconception that meditation means your mind has to be empty. Quite frankly our minds are always on, even when we sleep, so this is kind of unrealistic - especially for beginners.

What you can do is let the thoughts pass. Just let them come through without getting attached to them. I promise you that they do indeed pass and you will feel much better afterward. In fact, when that happens it's called an active meditation and many believe those fearful thoughts are coming up to be healed. Just let them pass.

The point here is to open up the right side of the brain which has the capacity to help you come up with creative solutions to your problems that the left side of your brain may not be getting. You'll also get insight and intuition starts kicking in.

For those of you who are completely new to this, relax, it's simple. Sit up straight, close your eyes, breathe in through your nose extending your belly outward, and then out through your mouth as you contract your belly. If your mind wanders just bring your focus back to your breath.

Some may even find it helpful to use a small mantra to focus the mind. Back in the day one of my yoga instructors recommended I say "So Hum" (I am that) as I breathed. As you inhale think "So" and as you exhale think "Hum." It works like a charm. I even use it to fall asleep sometimes if my mind happens to be particularly active.

I created some audio meditations to get you started/ You can also download the audio meditations at www.amandaabella.com/meditate. (Password: moneyhoney)

You can also check out my Meditation Motivation video on YouTube for some of my favorite resources. (www.youtube.com/user/amandaa3311)

Physical Reconditioning

One of the best ways to combat a mental shit storm is to move your body. If you've got a lot of stress and pent up frustration around the idea of money try something like kickboxing or HIIT. If you need to be a bit more passive, open up your body, and go with the flow try yoga.

Or you can also couple some financial themes with certain exercises. For instance, I got in the habit of doing tricep dips whenever I noticed a dip in the bank account. Much like seeing a dip in your finances, tricep dips are hard (and painful) but you always come back up.

Gratitude

Gratitude is such a solid way of getting grounded when you're elbow deep in a money storm. I do a gratitude list almost every morning or evening or I do a meditation to remind myself that I've got way more than enough.

In fact, the first thing I do upon waking up is start saying thanks. I'm half asleep and in my head I'm thinking "Thank you God for another day. Thank you for the sun. Thank you for a good night's sleep. Thank you for a roof over my head and food on the table. Thank you for all the examples of love in my life. Thank you for the money in the bank. And thank you for everything that is to come."

I'm saying thank you all day long. Nothing gets you grounded or attracts abundance quite like realizing all of the amazing things that are already present in your life.

Say thank you every time money comes in or every time you get a gift. In fact, if you really want to get radical and rock some gratitude start practicing while you are paying your bills.

Yes, you heard right. Practice some gratitude when money is going out the door. Hear me out. Every time I'm paying a bill I say "Thank you because I have the funds to cover this and I know there is more money on the way."

That is a sure fire way to start changing the way you see money! Works like a charm!

Practice Forgiveness

You may be wondering what the hell forgiveness has to do with money. Well, in my book, everything.

Remember that the topic of finances is very emotionally charged and we as society tend to put a lot of pressure on ourselves (and each other) to either keep up with the Jones' or have a spectacular financial portfolio.

In reality no one is perfect. We've all made mistakes with money. And we will probably at some point make mistakes with money when it comes to our businesses (some of you probably already have - I know I definitely have!). This can make us very fearful of spending money when we actually need to, take out our emotions on the credit card, stop us asking from what we are worth, and keep us from making better choices with our money.

To combat this I want you to practice forgiveness every time you find yourself making a money mistake - from feeling very anxious to having put a little bit too much on the credit card.

Trust me, forgiving yourself, letting it go, and allowing yourself to do better next time is way more effective than feeling guilty. Guilt only yields more guilt, which more often than not leads to acting out to avoid feeling it.

So go ahead. Give yourself a break. And breathe easy throughout your money process. Remember, this is a major practice that takes time to get used to, so allow yourself to get used to it. With time you'll find yourself bringing a new money story into all aspects of your business!

Watch Your Words

Words are powerful - really powerful. Countless studies have been done on the effect of words on energy and people, with the most famous one having been conducted by Masaru Emoto. Emoto's study exposed water in glasses to different words, pictures, or music. He then froze the water and studied the aesthetics of the resulting crystals.

The water that was exposed to happier words, music, or pictures had beautiful crystalline structures. Meanwhile, those that were exposed to things universally regarded as bad or negative had sporadic shapes and structure.

Doreen Virtue conducted a similar experiment with her son while they were recording podcasts. When they recorded words universally known as good and positive the recording graphics were wide and expansive. Meanwhile the opposite was true with the more negative words.

Moral of the story: watch how you talk about money. It does affect our energy levels and it most certainly affects our nervous system.

You may also realize you may need to distance yourself from people who are always complaining about money. Before we know it we're right in the story with them - even if it has nothing to do with us!

Lastly, you may want to stop watching the news. I used to say this all the time back when people would ask me what Gen Y should do to start getting their stuff together.

In case you haven't already noticed (though I'm sure you have) the news is pretty hyped up these days. Constantly hearing about how crappy the economy is or how messed up the world is certainly isn't going to help your case.

And no, you won't die or be any less of an informed citizen if you cut back on the news watching. You'll hear it through the grapevine or you can skim some headlines. If you must get some news then I highly recommend *The Skimm*. Their approach is fun, quick, and won't make you feel like you need to crawl under a rock.

I've taken all three of these steps and quickly found that it was easier to make and manage money when I wasn't caught up complaining about it, listening to others complain about it, or exposing myself to the national media complaining about it. In fact, I had two deals come through just writing this book and I do believe it a big part of that has to do with what words I've decided to use around the conversation of money.

Go on a Date with Your Budget

Making money your honey thing is a lot easier said than done - especially when it comes to finances because it's a story so deeply entrenched in our psyches. Lucky for you I'm all about putting this kind of principle into practical tools so here goes my favorite one:

Go on a date with your budget.

Your major assignment is to go on a romantic date with your budget. Let's be real here, talking about money can be incredibly uncomfortable. In fact, I'm pretty sure most people would rather talk about their sex lives. However, we all have to deal with money in this life so why not start treating it with some love?

Block out a few hours one afternoon (or night, or morning, whatever works for you) to take a very good look at your finances. Collect all of your bank statements and bills and become open to the idea of sorting through them carefully.

In order to do this I want you to create an environment where you are going to feel relaxed and comfortable. Dim the lights, light some candles, play music you dig, hang a "Do Not Disturb" sign on the door, and do whatever makes you feel most comfortable.

The more comfortable and relaxed you can make yourself the better. Bring that willingness from the previous step by stating "I am willing to see things differently. I am willing to change my money story" before you start.

Then, have at it! Take specific notes and what's coming and what's going out. You may notice that you can cut back on necessary spending, or you may notice that you need to raise your rates. You may come up with a plan for paying down debt. And above all - you're going to know exactly how much you need to make from your own business in order to make a living.

For very specific guidance my YouTube video, How to Go On a Date With Your Budget (www.youtube.com/users/amandaa331)

Here are the main things you want to look for:

- *How much money is coming in? (If you have a business and a day job separate the numbers by source of income.)*

- *How much is going out? What is it going out to? Are you leaking in too many places?*

- *Where can you cut costs?*

- *How much do you need to make to quit your job/cover your costs?*

- *How much do you WANT to make? (It may helpful to take an annual number and then split it by month.)*

- *What do you have in savings?*

- *Have you saved for taxes?*

- *How much do you owe and what are the payments? (Car loan, credit card debt, student loans)*

It is by getting down and dirty with our finances that we can actually see what is going on. It may be scary at first, but trust in

your commitment to cultivating a
relationship with your money.

Rather than ignoring credit card bills
take a deep breath, pour yourself a glass of
wine, and commit to some much needed
alone time with your budget. Do this once a
month and dealing with money is going to
start becoming a lot more fun.

Paying Yourself First

How often do we get paid and immediately run to pay all our bills? How often are we finding ourselves in this feast or famine cycle of varying income?

Yeah, I thought so.

You know what I think? I think its bullshit. I think this only perpetuates the idea that work and finances need to be difficult, scary, and ridden with anxiety. It's also in blatant contrast to taking care of ourselves so we can be of service to others.

The only way to combat this is to actually pay yourself first. You heard me, screw your bills when that PayPal alert comes through and take care of yourself first.

Here's how I break it down: whenever I get a deposit whether it's from writing, a coaching client, or commissions I break it down into different sections.

- **Taxes:** 15% (I live in Florida where there is no State Tax and have paid 15% on average in the past. You have to figure out your own situation. With deductions I usually end up saving way more than I need to, but it's better to cushion yourself. Furthermore, if you've been self-employed for more than a year you'll be paying your taxes quarterly in order to avoid any penalties. Your accountant can help you figure this out. So can most accounting and tax software.)

- **Business Checking:** 40% (for all of those business expenses that count as tax deductions)

- **Personal Checking:** 20% (For automatic retirement savings withdrawal, gym memberships, eating out with friends, rent, etc.)

- **Emergency Fund:** 10%

- **Big Expense:** 10% (For instance a car or a down payment on something)

- **Fun Money:** 5% (In a nutshell: shoes. I love shoes.)

You'll notice I've got a 60/40 split going on here. Sixty percent of whatever comes in goes to me and what I need to take care of. Forty percent of what comes in goes right back into my business and all that comes with it (phone bills, Skype, business meetings, trips, etc.)

I split this up IMMEDIATELY upon a deposit clearing in my bank account. Not after paying bills, not after paying off my credit card in full, and not after going on a shopping spree. All it takes it's some savings accounts and bank transfers.

This particular equation works for me, but it may not work for everyone depending on your financial situation. For instance, I don't have debt and I've managed to get my expenses pretty low. I've also gotten a very good handle on my spending since figuring out what I valued.

I was only able to figure out the proper equation AFTER I went on a date with my budget and figured out what the hell was going on and what patterns needed to change.

The point here isn't the equation. You could put 2% in an emergency fund instead of 10% and it will still make a huge difference in your financial life. The point here is that you partake in the action of taking care of yourself first.

The equation may vary (and believe me it has varied even for me) but the method is rock solid. I've been using this method for years and even recommend it to people who have regular fixed income from a full time job. It's been a great way of covering all of my bases, accounting for dips, paying my bills, and making sure I can still have some fun.

Figuring Out the Equation

I'm going to give you a really easy example to help you figure out your percentages. Once you've gone on a date with your budget you'll know how much money is coming in versus how much is going out.

For the sake of example let's say it's a 50/50 split between money you spend and money you get to keep. Split the money you get to keep into smaller percentages with their respective high yield savings account. For instance, 10% goes immediately into the account labeled "Emergency Fund."

Again, the percentage doesn't matter. Some of you may be thinking "Holy crap Amanda! Ten percent of my income going into an emergency fund? You're f***ing nuts!" That's cool because everyone's situation is different. Go with whatever feels most comfortable to you (maybe 3-5%) and make damn sure that money gets put away

before you even think about paying your
bills. You can then adjust it later when you
feel more comfortable.

Go Make That Money, Honey!

By this point you've started sorting through the mental cobwebs around the idea of money, even the sneaky ones! You've also gotten down and dirty with your numbers by going on a date with your budget and have learned about paying yourself first.

Now it's time to make that money, honey! The following questions will help you to not only figure out the dollars and cents of bringing in money through your business, but also help you notice any low hanging fruit you may be missing out on.

Where do you want this income to come from?

For instance I make the majority of my money from coaching and the rest comes from writing. I also have a small percentage that comes from affiliate sales. There's no need to drive yourself nuts with multiple sources of income at this time, just got for whatever is easiest for you.

Is there any low hanging fruit?

Did you forget to write an invoice? Is a payment late? Is there something you are really good at but aren't charging for? Is there an agreement that needs to be renewed? When I asked myself this question I realized I could write resumes in my sleep, so I started offering a resume writing service for those clients who were totally on board with my philosophy, but weren't quite ready to go into business full time yet.

It's an awesome feeling to know that even when my coaching income isn't as high as I'd like on any given month that I can easily make more money elsewhere. It really does give you peace of mind and helps you start trusting yourself more.

How many clients do you need on a monthly basis with your current pay structure?

Very important! You may realize that you either need to raise your rates or change your offerings.

Do you need to raise rates or change your offerings? How so?

Remember, it all goes back to providing value! What are you solving for people and what's it worth? It may also be helpful to recognize if maybe you need to be clearer about your current offerings. For instance, while I was constantly coaching people around their money fears it hadn't occurred to me to market myself in a way that represented that until I started writing this book.

And the big one, where are you going to find these people? How can you talk to them? What systems can you put in place to make it consistent? (You can go back to Section Two of this book to help you out!)

Money does not need to be scary. It's not the root of all evil, though our stories about it are certainly the root of several fears. You can always make more money and believe it or not there is abundance all around you.

You have skills that people will pay you for. You always have creative options; you just have to be open to them. Finally, you have to actually believe you deserve to be getting paid for the value you are putting forth into the world.

It's very easy to make yourself small here. Charge too little, put in too much work for no pay, and take our feelings out on our credit card. If this happens to you, just forgive yourself and do better next time. Practice the principles in this chapter every day and your disposition around money will naturally start to change - once that changes watch how it flows your way.

Conclusion

Back in March 2013 I had my first speaking gig and a good friend of mine was gracious enough to take pictures of the event for my website. After the event we were celebrating at a bar with a couple of other friends.

As he was flipping through the pictures in his camera he suddenly stopped and said "Look how happy you are in these pictures! You really love what you're doing, don't you?" It was at that moment when I realized I had it made. I replied with a resounding "Yes I do!" and took the energy in.

You can create the kind of work you actually get excited about in the morning.

You can have a beautiful relationship with your finances. You can significantly improve your quality of life any time you wish and it is my hope that you remember this throughout your career.

Thank you for listening to my story. I am truly grateful that I can share my story to help you all pursue your life's work, become financially savvy, and actually enjoy this one life we all have to live.

This journey to step into your own power with work and money isn't always easy, but it is well worth it. It took a Recession and years of overworking myself to realize things didn't have to be so damn difficult. It took a lot of inner work, research, experimenting, and working with others for me to realize that such uncomfortable topics didn't have to be so scary.

It is not easy to face your work life and your finances. We've been conditioned to think that these topics are meant to be ridden with struggle for them to be of any merit.

I call bullshit.

Work and money can be beautiful romances and all you have to do is make the choice to see them that way. Just remember you always have the ability to see things in a better light and no one can ever take that away from you.

It may be kind of weird at first, especially because we're so deeply programmed to think otherwise, but with daily practice I promise it starts becoming second nature until one day it's a no brainer.

Come from a place of service, value what you bring to the table, and treat your money with the same care and respect you would treat your own body.

I use the suggestions in this book whenever I need them and it is my hope that you come back to it again and again whenever you need a tune up.

If you get only one thing from this book I hope it's this:

Only you have the real power to create the kind of career you want with a bank account to match. And only you can make the decisions that will lead to the kind of life you've always wanted.

Not your spouse, not your clients, and certainly not an economic recession.

Amanda Abella

Acknowledgements

Thank you to all of the incredible people in my life.

My Parents: For believing in this probably even more than I do. Most parents would have told their kids to go to law school, you told me to screw that and create my own fulfilling career. For that I am eternally grateful.

My Brother: For taking my very first pictures with a taped up camera, running around Europe with me, having better taste in music than most people I know, and being the only person that I can be my fully silly self with (even when you make fun of me).

My Friends: For being just as crazy as I am. For showing up to speaking gigs, buying me tequila when something doesn't work out, handing me books that change my life, constantly teaching me new things that improve my quality of life and all the good times. Thank you for being as optimistic about life as I am.

My Coach: Jennie Mustafa-Julock, I would not be where I am without your audacious cathartic shoves and constant support. Thanks for believing in me even when I couldn't see it myself just yet. Thank you for constantly pushing me out of my comfort zone and calling me out on my bullshit :)

My Former Boss: Thank you for hiring me and teaching me so much about what it takes to run a business. I meant it when I said I didn't need an MBA because you were my boss. You didn't just give me a job; you gave me an education that will last me a lifetime.

My Colleagues: There are more of you than I can count! You're not just colleagues, you're friends and family. People who are doing all they can to change the world in their own way. You are a constant inspiration in my life! Special thanks to Rachael Kay Albers for undertaking my major site and company re-brand and Brandy Morris for helping me realize this book was the right move for my business. Also a special thanks to Diana Antholis for taking the time to talk with me about actually getting this puppy out into the world! Thanks to all the bloggers I've met online and at conferences for sharing your knowledge with the world.

My Community: To all of my clients, readers, subscribers and social media followers; I could not have done any of this without you.

About the Author

Amanda Abella is the founder of former Gen Y blog Grad Meets World and creator of the lifestyle brand AmandaAbella.com

As a writer, motivational speaker, and certified life coach she helps creative and soulful entrepreneurs create the businesses and lives they love. Her ability to combine traditional forms of coaching with her career consulting background and fiery creative spirit has helped clients change their lives by creating fulfilling work and owning their power as women and entrepreneurs.

Her approach is simple: create work that fits seamlessly into your life. Work,

money and life don't have to be at odds with
each other. She also believes in creating
tangible steps that are easy and fun to
implement into business and life.

Her background in recruiting for
Fortune 500 companies as well as her own
struggles with being a post-grad professional
during the Great Recession led her to
experience firsthand that many people's
views on work and money were negatively
affecting every other area of their lives. As
she developed her own tools and resources
for creating her own sacred business, she
gave up the 9 to 5 gig to help others create
their own beautiful work and feel better
about money.

Amanda is a certified professional
coach through the International Coaching
Academy and actively pursues other
personal development certifications. She
also holds a bachelor's degree in English
Literature from Ave Maria University.

She runs the popular blog on
AmandaAbella.com and has been featured in
*Forbes, Kiplinger, Huffington Post Live,
The Chicago Tribune,* and more. She is an
assistant editor for *Miami on the Cheap,* a
South Florida based deals and personal
finance site and runs *The Miami Herald's*
FruGal blog. She is also a financial
education blogger for *The Huffington Post.*

She has also spoken nationally for organizations and conferences including *The Levo League's Local Levo Miami, Women of Tomorrow,* and *The Financial Blogger Conference.*

Resources & Extra Support

It is my hope that you use this guide again and again as you embark on your own magical journey of work and money. Should you need any extra support or one-on-one guidance implementing the principles in this book feel free to book yourself a free Fire Up Your Biz session by visiting my website or emailing me at amanda@amandaabella.com

How-tos, workshops, and blog posts on work, money, health, creating your best life, and more.

http://www.amandaabella.com

Free Fire Tribe Membership

Free access to full length video workshop and 30-day action plan Set Fire to Your Goals.

http://www.amandaabella.com/join-the-tribe

Private FIRE Coaching Program

http://www.amandaabella.com/coaching

Facebook Fireballs Facebook Group

https://www.facebook.com/groups/fireballambassadors/

Free Downloadable Guided Audio Meditations

Password: moneyhoney

http://www.amandaabella.com/meditate/

Instructional YouTube Videos

http://www.youtube.com/user/amandaa3311

Made in the USA
Lexington, KY
12 February 2014